THE VEDANTA PHILOSOPHY

This edition published by Lector House in 2024

ISBN: 978-93-6138-017-4

Lector House LLP
Registered Office: H. No. 96, Block C, Tomar Colony,
Burari, Delhi – 110084, India
info@lectorhouse.com
www.lectorhouse.com

THE VEDANTA PHILOSOPHY

SWAMI VIVEKANANDA

2024

LECTOR HOUSE

LECTOR HOUSE LLP

Swami Vivekananda

THE VEDANTA PHILOSOPHY

An Address before the
Graduate Philosophical Society
of
Harvard University
March 25, 1896

BY THE

SWAMI VIVEKANANDA

WITH AN INTRODUCTION BY
CHARLES CARROLL EVERETT, D.D., LL.D.

Contents

Introduction

The Swami Vivekananda was sent by his friends and co-religionists to present their belief at the Congress of Religions that was held in connection with the World's Fair in Chicago. This he did in a way to win general interest and admiration. Since then he has lectured on the same theme in different parts of our country. He has been in fact a missionary from India to America. Everywhere he has made warm personal friends; and his expositions of Hindu philosophy have been listened to with delight. It is very pleasant to observe the eager interest with which his own people in India follow his course, and the joy that they take in his success. I have seen a pamphlet filled with speeches made at a large and influential meeting in Calcutta, which was called together to express enthusiastic approval of the manner in which he has fulfilled his mission; and satisfaction at this invasion of the West by oriental thought. This satisfaction is well grounded. We may not be so near to actual conversion as some of these speakers seem to believe; but Vivekananda has created a high degree of interest in himself and his work. There are indeed few departments of study more attractive than the Hindu thought. It is a rare pleasure to see a form of belief that to most seems so far away and unreal as the Vedanta system, represented by an actually living and extremely intelligent believer. This system is not to be regarded merely as a curiosity, as a speculative vagary. Hegel said that Spinozism is the necessary beginning of all philosophising. This can be said even more emphatically of the Vedanta system. We occidentals busy ourselves with the manifold. We can, however, have no understanding of the manifold, if we have no sense of the One in which the manifold exists. The reality of the One is the truth which the East may well teach us; and we owe a debt of gratitude to Vivekananda that he has taught this lesson so effectively.

C. C. EVERETT.

HARVARD UNIVERSITY.

Note

This lecture and the discussion which followed were stenographically reported. They could receive from the Swami only a cursory revision, owing to his departure for England; but it is hoped no errors have crept in. Professor LANMAN and Professor WRIGHT of Harvard have kindly assisted in the final revision. In the reporting of the discussion, some of the questions were unavoidably lost. The first four notes were added by the Swami. In the original lecture, the quotations from Hindu writings were first given in the Sanskrit, and then translated; these off-hand translations stand as given.

Following the lecture and discussion, are the answers of the Swami to questions at two afternoon talks with some Harvard students, on March 22 and 24. These answers were stenographically reported, but the questions were not. There have also been added a few selections from unpublished lectures. Some of the answers and selections cover the same general ground, but they have all been retained on account of the variety in treatment. While no adequate exposition of the Vedānta philosophy can be given in a single address, it is hoped that this, with the accompanying answers and selections, will be of value to those interested in the thought and life of the East.

J. P. F.

The Vedanta Philosophy

The Vedānta philosophy, as it is generally called at the present day, really comprises all the various sects that now exist in India. Thus there have been various interpretations, and to my mind they have been progressive, beginning with the dualistic or Dvaita and ending with the non-dualistic or Advaita. The word *Vedānta* literally means the end of the Vedas—the Vedas being the scriptures of the Hindus.[1] Sometimes in the West by the Vedas are meant only the hymns and rituals of the Vedas. But at the present time these parts have almost gone out of use, and usually by the word *Vedas* in India, the Vedānta is meant. All our commentators, when they want to quote a passage from the scriptures, as a rule, quote from the Vedānta, which has another technical name with the commentators—the Shrutis.[2] Now, all the books known by the name of the Vedānta were not entirely written after the ritualistic portions of the Vedas.

[1] The Vedas are divided mainly into two portions: the Karmakānda and the Jnāna-kānda—the work-portion and the knowledge-portion. To the Karma-kānda belong the famous hymns and the rituals of Brāhmanas. Those books which treat of spiritual matters apart from ceremonials are called Upanishads. The Upanishads belong to the Jnāna-kānda, or knowledge-portion. It is not that all the Upanishads were composed as a separate portion of the Vedas. Some are interspersed among the rituals, and at least one is in the Samhitā, or hymn-portion. Sometimes the term *Upanishad* is applied to books which are not included in the Vedas—e.g. the Gitā; but as a rule it is applied to the philosophical treatises scattered through the Vedas. These treatises have been collected, and are called the Vedānta.

[2] The term Shruti—meaning "that which is heard"—though including the whole of the Vedic literature, is chiefly applied by the commentators to the Upanishads.

For instance, one of them—the Ishā Upanishad—forms the fortieth chapter of the Yajur-veda, that being one of the oldest parts of the Vedas. There are other Upanishads[3] which form portions of the Brāhmanas or ritualistic writings; and the rest of the Upanishads are independent, not comprised in any of the Brāhmanas or other parts of the Vedas; but there is no reason to suppose that they were entirely independent of other parts, for, as we well know, many of these have been lost entirely and many of the Brāhmanas have become extinct. So it is quite possible that the independent Upanishads belonged to some Brāhmanas, which in course of time fell into disuse, while the Upanishads remained. These Upanishads are also called Forest Books or Āranyakas.

The Vedānta, then, practically forms the scriptures of the Hindus, and all systems of philosophy that are orthodox have to take it as their foundation. Even the Buddhists and Jains, when it suits their purpose, will quote a passage from the Vedānta as authority. All schools of philosophy in India, although they claim to have been based upon the Vedas, took different names for their systems. The last one, the system of Vyāsa, took its stand upon the doctrines of the Vedas more than the previous systems did, and made an attempt to harmonise the preceding philosophies, such as the Sānkhya and the Nyāya, with the doctrines of the Vedānta. So it is especially called the Vedānta philosophy; and the Sutras or aphorisms of Vyāsa are, in modern India, the basis of the Vedānta philosophy. Again, these Sutras of Vyāsa have been variously explained by different commentators. In general there are three sorts of commentators[4]

---

[3] The Upanishads are said to be one hundred and eight in number. Their dates cannot be fixed with certainty—only it is certain that they are older than the Buddhistic movement. Though some of the minor Upanishads contain allusions indicating a later date, yet that does not prove the later date of the treatise, as in very many cases in Sanskrit literature, the substance of a book, though of very ancient date, receives a coating, as it were, of later events in the hands of the sectarians, to exalt their particular sect.

[4] The commentaries are of various sorts such as the Bhāshya, Tikā, Tippani, Churni, etc., of which all except the Bhāshya are explanations of the text or difficult words in the text. The Bhashya is not properly a commentary, but the elucidātion of a system of philosophy out of texts, the

in India now; from their interpretations have arisen three systems of philosophy and sects. One is dualistic, or Dvaita; a second is the qualified non-dualistic, or Vishishtādvaita; and a third is the non-dualistic, or Advaita. Of these the dualistic and the qualified non-dualistic include the largest number of the Indian people. The non-dualists are comparatively few in number. Now I will try to lay before you the ideas that are contained in all these three sects; but before going on, I will make one remark—that these different Vedānta systems have one common psychology, and that is, the psychology of the Sānkhya system. The Sānkhya psychology is very much like the psychologies of the Nyāya and Vaisheshika systems, differing only in minor particulars.

All the Vedantists agree on three points. They believe in God, in the Vedas as revealed, and in cycles. We have already considered the Vedas. The belief about cycles is as follows: All matter throughout the universe is the outcome of one primal matter called Ākāsha; and all force, whether gravitation, attraction or repulsion, or life, is the outcome of one primal force called Prāna. Prāna acting on Ākāsha is creating or projecting[5] the universe. At the beginning of a cycle,

---

object being not to explain the words, but to bring out a philosophy. So the writer of a Bhashya expands his own system, taking texts as authorities for his system.

There have been various commentaries on the Vedānta. Its doctrines found their final expression in the philosophical aphorisms of Vyāsa. This treatise, called the Uttara Mimāmsā, is the standard authority of Vedantism—nay, is the most authoritative exposition of the Hindu scriptures. The most antagonistic sects have been compelled, as it were, to take up the texts of Vyāsa, and harmonise them with their own philosophy. Even in very ancient times the commentators on the Vedānta philosophy formed themselves into the three celebrated Hindu sects of dualists, qualified non-dualists, and non-dualists. The ancient commentaries are perhaps lost; but they have been revived in modern times by the post-Buddhistic commentators, Shankara, Rāmānuja, and Madhva. Shankara revived the non-dualistic form; Rāmānuja, the qualified non-dualistic form of the ancient commentator Bodhāyana; and Madhva, the dualistic form. In India the sects differ mainly in their philosophy; the difference in rituals is slight, the basis of their philosophy and religion being the same.

[5] The word which is "creation" in the English language is in Sanskrit

Ākāsha is motionless, unmanifested. Then Prāna begins to act, more and more, creating grosser and grosser forms out of Ākāsha—plants, animals, men, stars, and so on. After an incalculable time this evolution ceases and involution begins, everything being resolved back through finer and finer forms into the original Ākāsha and Prāna, when a new cycle follows. Now there is something beyond Ākāsha and Prāna. Both can be resolved into a third thing called Mahat—the Cosmic Mind. This Cosmic Mind does not create Ākāsha and Prāna, but changes itself into them.

We will now take up the beliefs about mind, soul, and God. According to the universally accepted Sānkhya psychology, in perception—in the case of vision, for instance—there are, first of all, the instruments of vision, the eyes. Behind the instruments—the eyes—is the organ of vision or Indriya—the optic nerve and its centres—which is not the external instrument, but without which the eyes will not see. More still is needed for perception. The mind or Manas must come and attach itself to the organ. And besides this, the sensation must be carried to the intellect or Buddhi—the determinative, reactive state of the mind. When the reaction comes from Buddhi, along with it flashes the external world and egoism. Here then is the will; but everything is not complete. Just as every picture, being composed of successive impulses of light, must be united on something stationary to form a whole, so all the ideas in the mind must be gathered and projected on something that is stationary—relatively to the body and mind—that is, on what is called the Soul or Purusha or Ātman.

According to the Sānkhya philosophy, the reactive state of the mind called Buddhi or intellect is the outcome, the change, or a certain manifestation of the Mahat or Cosmic Mind. The Mahat becomes changed into vibrating thought; and that becomes in one part changed into the organs, and in the other part into the fine particles of matter. Out of the combination of all these, the whole of this universe, from Mahat down to the grossest objects, is produced.

---

exactly "projection," because there is no sect in India which believes in creation as it is regarded in the West—a something coming out of nothing. What we mean by creation is projection of that which already existed. (The Ātman, p. 9.)

Behind even Mahat, the Sānkhya conceives of a certain state which is called Avyakta or unmanifested, where even the manifestation of mind is not present, but only the causes exist. It is also called Prakriti. Beyond this Prakriti, and eternally separate from it, is the Purusha, the soul of the Sānkhya which is without attributes and omnipresent. The Purusha is not the doer but the witness. The illustration of the crystal is used to explain the Purusha. The latter is said to be like a crystal without any colour, before which different colours are placed, and then it seems to be coloured by all the colours before it, but in reality it is not. The Vedantists reject the Sānkhya ideas of the soul and nature. They claim that between them there is a huge gulf to be bridged over. On the one hand the Sānkhya system comes to nature, and then at once it has to jump over to the other side and come to the soul, which is entirely separate from nature. How can these different colours, as Sānkhya calls them, be able to act on that soul which by its nature is colourless? So the Vedantists, from the very first, affirm that this soul and this nature are one.[6] Even the dualistic Vedantists admit that the Ātman or God is not only the efficient cause of this universe, but also the material cause. But they only say so in so many words. They do not really mean it, for they try to escape from their conclusions, in this way. They say there are three existences in this universe—God, soul, and nature. Nature and soul are, as it were, the body of God, and in this sense it may be said that God and the whole universe are one. But this nature and all these various souls remain different from each other through all eternity. Only at the beginning of a cycle do they become manifest; and when the cycle ends, they become fine, and remain in a fine state. The Advaita Vedantists—the non-dualists—reject this theory of the soul, and, having nearly the whole range of the Upanishads in their favour, build their philosophy entirely upon them. All the books contained in the Upanishads have one subject, one task before them—to prove the following theme:

[6] The Vedānta and the Sānkhya philosophy are very little opposed to each other. The Vedānta God developed out of the Sānkhya's Purusha. All the systems take up the psychology of the Sānkhya. Both the Vedānta and the Sānkhya believe in the infinite soul; only the Sānkhya believes there are many souls. According to the Sānkhya, this universe does not require any explanation from outside. The Vedānta believes that there is the one Soul, which appears as many; and we build on the Sānkhya's analysis. (Talk of March 24, 1896.)

"Just as by the knowledge of one lump of clay we have the knowledge of all the clay in the universe, so what is that, knowing which we know everything in the universe?" The idea of the Advaitists is to generalise the whole universe into one—that something which is really the whole of this universe. And they claim that this whole universe is one, that it is one Being manifesting itself in all these various forms. They admit that what the Sānkhya calls nature exists, but say that nature is God. It is this Being, the Sat, which has become converted into all this—the universe, man, soul, and everything that exists. Mind and Mahat are but the manifestations of that one Sat. But then the difficulty arises that this would be pantheism. How came that Sat which is unchangeable, as they admit (for that which is absolute is unchangeable), to be changed into that which is changeable, and perishable? The Advaitists here have a theory which they call Vivarta-vāda or apparent manifestation. According to the dualists and the Sānkhyas, the whole of this universe is the evolution of primal nature. According to some of the Advaitists and some of the dualists, the whole of this universe is evolved from God. And according to the Advaitists proper, the followers of Shankarāchārya, the whole universe is the *apparent* evolution of God. God is the material cause of this universe, but not really, only apparently. The celebrated illustration used is that of the rope and the snake, where the rope appeared to be the snake, but was not really so. The rope did not really change into the snake. Even so this whole universe as it exists is that Being. It is unchanged, and all the changes we see in it are only apparent. These changes are caused by Desha, Kāla, and Nimitta (space, time, and causation), or, according to a higher psychological generalisation, by Nāma and Rupa (name and form). It is by name and form that one thing is differentiated from another. The name and form alone cause the difference. In reality they are one and the same. Again, it is not, the Vedantists say, that there is something as phenomenon and something as noumenon. The rope is changed into the snake apparently only; and when the delusion ceases, the snake vanishes. When one is in ignorance, he sees the phenomenon and does not see God. When he sees God, this universe vanishes entirely for him. Ignorance or Māyā, as it is called, is the cause of all this phenomenon—the Absolute, the Unchangeable, being taken as this manifested universe. This Māyā is not absolute zero, nor non-existence. It is defined as neither existence nor non-existence. It is not existence, because that can be said only of the Absolute, the Unchangeable, and in this sense, Māyā is non-existence. Again, it cannot be said it is non-existence; for if it were, it could never produce the phenomenon. So it is something which is neither; and in the Vedānta philosophy it is called Anirvachaniya or inexpressible. Māyā, then, is the real cause of this universe. Māyā gives the name and form to what Brahman or God gives the material; and the latter seems to have been transformed into all this. The Advaitists, then have no place for the individual soul. They say individual souls are created by Māyā. In reality they cannot exist. If there were only one existence throughout, how could it be that I am one, and you are one, and so forth? We are all one, and the cause of evil is the perception of duality. As soon as I begin to feel that I am separate from this universe, then first comes fear, and then comes misery. "Where one hears another, one sees another, that is small. Where one does not see another, where one does not hear another, that is the greatest, that is God. In that greatest is perfect happiness. In small things there is no happiness."

According to the Advaita philosophy, then, this differentiation of matter, these phenomena, are, as it were, for a time, hiding the real nature of man; but the latter really has not been changed at all. In the lowest worm, as well as in the highest human being, the same divine nature is present. The worm form is the lower form in which the divinity has been more overshadowed by Māyā; that is the highest form in which it has been least overshadowed. Behind everything the same divinity is existing, and out of this comes the basis of morality. Do not injure another. Love everyone as your own self, because the whole universe is one. In injuring another, I am injuring myself; in loving another, I am loving myself. From this also springs that principle of Advaita morality which has been summed up in one word—self-abnegation. The Advaitist says, this little personalised self is the cause of all my misery. This individualised self, which makes me different from all other beings, brings hatred and jealousy and misery, struggle and all other evils. And when this idea has been got rid of, all struggle will cease, all misery vanish. So this is to be given up. We must always hold ourselves ready, even to give up our lives for the lowest beings. When a man has become ready even to give up his life for a little insect, he has reached the perfection which the Advaitist wants to attain; and at that moment when he has become thus ready, the veil of ignorance falls away from him, and he will feel his own nature. Even in this life, he will feel that he is one with the universe. For a time, as it were, the whole of this phenomenal world will disappear for him, and he will realise what he is. But so long as the Karma of this body remains, he will have to live. This state, when the veil has vanished and yet the body remains for some time, is what the Vedantists call the Jivanmukti, the living freedom. If a man is deluded by a mirage for some time, and one day the mirage disappears—if it comes back again the next day, or at some future time, he will not be deluded. Before the mirage first broke, the man could not distinguish between the reality and the deception. But when it has once broken, as long as he has organs and eyes to work with, he will see the image, but will no more be deluded. That fine distinction between the actual world and the mirage he has caught, and the latter cannot delude him any more. So when the Vedantist has realised his own nature, the whole world has vanished for him. It will come back again, but no more the same world of misery. The prison of misery has become changed into Sat, Chit, Ānanda—Existence Absolute, Knowledge Absolute, Bliss Absolute—and the attainment of this is the goal of the Advaita Philosophy.

Discussion.

Q.—I should like to know something about the present activity of philosophic thought in India. To what extent are these questions discussed?

A.—As I have said, the majority of the Indian people are practically dualists, and the minority are monists. The main subject of discussion is Māyā and Jiva. When I came to this country, I found that the labourers were informed of the present condition of politics; but when I asked them, "What is religion, and what are the doctrines of this and that particular sect?" they said, "We do not know; we go to church." In India if I go to a peasant and ask him, "Who governs you?" he says, "I do not know; I pay my taxes." But if I ask him what is his religion, he says, "I am a dualist", and is ready to give you the details about Māyā and Jiva. He cannot read or write, but he has learned all this from the monks and is very fond of discussing it. After the day's work, the peasants sit under a tree and discuss these questions.

Q.—What does orthodoxy mean with the Hindus?

A.—In modern times it simply means obeying certain caste laws as to eating, drinking, and marriage. After that the Hindu can believe in any system he likes. There was never an organised church in India; so there was never a body of men to formulate doctrines of orthodoxy. In a general way, we say that those who believe in the Vedas are orthodox; but in reality we find that many of the dualistic sects believe more in the Purānas[7] than in the Vedas alone.

Q.—What influence had your Hindu philosophy on the Stoic philosophy of the Greeks?

A.—It is very probable that it had some influence on it through the Alexandrians. There is some suspicion of Pythagoras' being influenced by the Sānkhya thought. Anyway, we think the Sānkhya philosophy is the first attempt to harmonise the philosophy of the Vedas through reason. We find Kapila mentioned even in the Vedas:"**ऋषि प्रसूतं कपिलं यस्तमग्रे**—He who (supports through knowledge) the first-born sage Kapila."

Q.—What is the antagonism of this thought with Western science?

A.—No antagonism at all. We are in harmony with it. Our theory of evolution and of Ākāsha and Prāna is exactly what your modern philosophies have. Your belief in evolution is among our Yogis and in the Sānkhya philosophy. For instance, Patanjali speaks of one species being changed into another by the infilling of nature—"**जात्यन्तरपरिणामः प्रकृत्यापूरात्**"; only he differs from you in the explanation. His explanation of this evolution is spiritual. He says that just as when a farmer wants to water his field from the canals that pass near, he has only to lift up his gate—"**निमित्तमप्रयोजकं प्रकृतीनां वरणभेदस्तु ततः क्षेत्रिकवत्**"—so each man is the Infinite already, only these bars and bolts and different circumstances shut him in; but as soon as they are removed, he rushes out and expresses himself. In the animal, the man was held in abeyance; but as soon as good circumstances came, he was manifested as man. And again, as soon as fitting circumstances came, the God in man manifested itself. So we have very little to quarrel with in the new theories. For instance, the theory of the Sānkhya as to perception is very little different from modern physiology.

[7] Purānas, "old things,"—popular explanations of the Vedas.

Q.—But your method is different?

A.—Yes. We claim that concentrating the powers of the mind is the only way to knowledge. In external science, concentration of mind is—putting it on something external; and in internal science, it is—drawing towards one's Self. We call this concentration of mind Yoga.

Q.—In the state of concentration does the truth of these principles become evident?

A.—The Yogis claim a good deal. They claim that by concentration of the mind every truth in the universe becomes evident to the mind, both external and internal truth.

Q.—What does the Advaitist think of cosmology?

A.—The Advaitist would say that all this cosmology and everything else are only in Māyā, in the phenomenal world. In truth they do not exist. But as long as we are bound, we have to see these visions. Within these visions things come in a certain regular order. Beyond them there is no law and order, but freedom.

Q.—Is the Advaita antagonistic to dualism?

A.—The Upanishads not being in a systematised form, it was easy for philosophers to take up texts when they liked to form a system. The Upanishads had always to be taken, else there would be no basis. Yet we find all the different schools of thought in the Upaṇishads. Our solution is that the Advaita is not antagonistic to the Dvaita (dualism). We say the latter is only one of three steps. Religion always takes three steps. The first is dualism. Then man gets to a higher state, partial non-dualism. And at last he finds he is one with the universe. Therefore the three do not contradict but fulfil.

Q.—Why does Māyā or ignorance exist?

A.—"Why" cannot be asked beyond the limit of causation. It can only be asked within Māyā. We say we will answer the question when it is logically formulated. Before that we have no right to answer.

Q.—Does the Personal God belong to Māyā?

A.—Yes; but the Personal God is the same Absolute seen through Māyā. That Absolute under the control of nature is what is called the human soul; and that which is controlling nature is Ishvara, or the Personal God. If a man starts from here to see the sun, he will see at first a little sun; but as he proceeds he will see it bigger and bigger, until he reaches the real one. At each stage of his progress he was seeing apparently a different sun; yet we are sure it was the same sun he was seeing. So all these things are but visions of the Absolute, and as such they are true. Not one is a false vision, but we can only say they were lower stages.

Q.—What is the special process by which one will come to know the Absolute?

A.—We say there are two processes. One is the positive, and the other, the negative. The positive is that through which the whole universe is going—that of love. If this circle of love is increased indefinitely, we reach the one universal love. The other is the "Neti", "Neti"—"not this", "not this"—stopping every wave in the mind which tries to draw it out; and at last the mind dies, as it were, and the Real discloses Itself. We call that Samādhi, or superconsciousness.

Q.—That would be, then, merging the subject in the object!

A.—Merging the object in the subject, not merging the subject in the object. Really this world dies, and I remain. I am the only one that remains.

Q.—Some of our philosophers in Germany have thought that the whole doctrine of Bhakti (Love for the Divine) in India was very likely the result of occidental influence.

A.—I do not take any stock in that—the assumption was ephemeral. The Bhakti of India is not like the Western Bhakti. The central idea of ours is that there is no thought of fear. It is always, love God. There is no worship through fear, but always through love, from beginning to end. In the second place, the assumption is quite unnecessary. Bhakti is spoken of in the oldest of the Upanishads, which is much older than the Christian Bible. The germs of Bhakti are even in the Samhitā (the Vedic hymns). The word *Bhakti* is not a Western word. It was suggested by the word *Shraddhā*.

Q.—What is the Indian idea of the Christian faith?

A.—That it is very good. The Vedānta will take in every one. We have a peculiar idea in India. Suppose I had a child. I should not teach him any religion; I should teach him breathings—the practice of concentrating the mind, and just one line of prayer—not prayer in your sense, but simply something like this, "I meditate on Him who is the Creator of this universe: may He enlighten my mind!" That way he would be educated, and then go about hearing different philosophers and teachers. He would select one who, he thought, would suit him best; and this man would become his Guru or teacher, and he would become a Shishya or disciple. He would say to that man, "This form of philosophy which you preach is the best; so teach me." Our fundamental idea is that your doctrine cannot be mine, or mine yours. Each one must have his own way. My daughter may have one method, and my son another, and I again another. So each one has an Ishta or chosen way, and we keep it to ourselves. It is between me and my teacher, because we do not want to create a fight. It will not help any one to tell it to others, because each one will have to find his own way. So only general philosophy and general methods can be taught universally. For instance, giving a ludicrous example, it may help me to stand on one leg. It would be ludicrous to you if I said every one must do that, but it may suit me. It is quite possible for me to be a dualist and for my wife to be a monist, and so on. One of my sons may worship Christ or Buddha or Mohammed, so long as he obeys the caste laws. That is his own Ishta.

Q.—Do all Hindus believe in caste?

A.—They are forced to. They may not believe, but they have to obey.

Q.—Are these exercises in breathing and concentration universally practised?

A.—Yes; only some practise only a little, just to satisfy the requirements of their religion. The temples in India are not like the churches here. They may all vanish tomorrow, and will not be missed. A temple is built by a man who wants to go to heaven, or to get a son, or something of that sort. So he builds a large temple and employs a few priests to hold services there. I need not go there at all, because all my worship is in the home. In every house is a special room set apart, which is called the chapel. The first duty of the child, after his initiation, is to take a bath, and then to worship; and his worship consists of this breathing and meditating and repeating of a certain name. And another thing is to hold the body straight. We believe that the mind has every power over the body to keep it healthy. After one has done this, then another comes and takes his seat, and each one does it in silence. Sometimes there are three or four in the same room, but each one may have a different method. This worship is repeated at least twice a day.

Q.—This state of oneness that you speak of, is it an ideal or something actually attained?

A.—We say it is within actuality; we say we realise that state. If it were only in talk, it would be nothing. The Vedas teach three things: this Self is first to be heard, then to be reasoned, and then to be meditated upon. When a man first hears it, he must reason on it, so that he does not believe it ignorantly, but knowingly; and after reasoning what it is, he must meditate upon it, and then realise it. And that is religion. Belief is no part of religion. We say religion is a superconscious state.

Q.—If you ever reach that state of superconsciousness, can you ever tell about it?

A.—No; but we know it by its fruits. An idiot, when he goes to sleep, comes out of sleep an idiot or even worse. But another man goes into the state of meditation, and when he comes out he is a philosopher, a sage, a great man. That shows the difference between these two states.

Q.—I should like to ask, in continuation of Professor's question, whether you know of any people who have made any study of the principles of self-hypnotism, which they undoubtedly practised to a great extent in ancient India, and what has been recently stated and practised in that thing. Of course you do not have it so much in modern India.

A.—What you call hypnotism in the West is only a part of the real thing. The Hindus call it self-hypnotisation. They say you are hypnotised already, and that you should get out of it and de-hypnotise yourself. "There the sun cannot illume, nor the moon, nor the stars; the flash of lightning cannot illume that; what to speak of this mortal fire! That shining, everything else shines" (Katha Upanishad, II.ii.15). That is not hypnotisation, but de-hypnotisation. We say that every other religion that preaches these things as real is practising a form of hypnotism. It is the Advaitist alone that does not care to be hypnotised. His is the only system that more or less understands that hypnotism comes with every form of dualism. But the Advaitist says, throw away even the Vedas, throw away even the Personal God, throw away even the universe, throw away even your own body and mind, and let nothing remain, in order to get rid of hypnotism perfectly. "From where the mind comes back with speech, being unable to reach, knowing the Bliss of Brahman, no more is fear." That is de-hypnotisation. "I have neither vice nor virtue, nor misery nor happiness; I care neither for the Vedas nor sacrifices nor ceremonies; I am neither food nor eating nor eater, for I am Existence Absolute, Knowledge Absolute, Bliss Absolute; I am He, I am He." We know all about hypnotism. We have a psychology which the West is just beginning to know, but not yet adequately, I am sorry to say.

Q.—What do you call the astral body?

A.—The astral body is what we call the Linga Sharira. When this body dies, how can it come to take another body? Force cannot remain without matter. So a little part of the fine matter remains, through which the internal organs make another body—for each one is making his own body; it is the mind that makes the body. If I become a sage, my brain gets changed into a sage's brain; and the Yogis say that even in this life a Yogi can change his body into a god-body.

The Yogis show many wonderful things. One ounce of practice is worth a thousand pounds of theory. So I have no right to say that because I have not seen this or that thing done, it is false. Their books say that with practice you can get all sorts of results that are most wonderful. Small results can be obtained in a short time by regular practice, so that one may know that there is no humbug about it, no charlatanism. And these Yogis explain the very wonderful things mentioned in all scriptures in a scientific way. The question is, how these records of miracles entered into every nation. The man, who says that they are all false and need no explanation, is not rational. You have no right to deny them until you can prove them false. You must prove that they are without any foundation, and only then have you the right to stand up and deny them. But you have not done that. On the other hand, the Yogis say they are not miracles, and they claim that they can do them even today. Many wonderful things are done in India today. But none of them are done by miracles. There are many books on the subject. Again, if nothing else has been done in that line except a scientific approach towards psychology, that credit must be given to the Yogis.

Q.—Can you say in the concrete what the manifestations are which the Yogi can show?

A.—The Yogi wants no faith or belief in his science but that which is given to any other science, just enough gentlemanly faith to come and make the experiment. The ideal of the Yogi is tremendous. I have seen the lower things that can be done by the power of the mind, and therefore, I have no right to disbelieve that the highest things can be done. The ideal of the Yogi is eternal peace and love through omniscience and omnipotence. I know a Yogi who was bitten by a cobra, and who fell down on the ground. In the evening he revived again, and when asked what happened, he said: "A messenger came from my Beloved." All hatred and anger and jealousy have been burnt out of this man. Nothing can make him react; he is infinite love all the time, and he is omnipotent in his power of love. That is the real Yogi. And this manifesting different things is accidental on the way. That is not what he wants to attain. The Yogi says, every man is a slave except the Yogi. He is a slave of food, to air, to his wife, to his children, to a dollar, slave to a nation, slave to name and fame, and to a thousand things in this world. The man who is not controlled by any one of these bondages is alone a real man, a real Yogi. "They have conquered relative existence in this life who are firm-fixed in sameness. God is pure and the same to all. Therefore such are said to be living in God." (Gitā, V.19).

Q.—Do the Yogis attach any importance to caste?

A.—No; caste is only the training school for undeveloped minds.

Q.—Is there no connection between this idea of superconsciousness and the heat of India?

A.—I do not think so; because all this philosophy was thought out fifteen thousand feet above the level of the sea, among the Himalayas, in an almost Arctic temperature.

Q.—Is it practicable to attain success in a cold climate?

A.—It is practicable, and the only thing that is practicable in this world. We say you are a born Vedantist, each one of you. You are declaring your oneness with everything each moment you live. Every time that your heart goes out towards the world, you are a true Vedantist, only you do not know it. You are moral without knowing why; and the Vedānta is the philosophy which analysed and taught man to be moral consciously. It is the essence of all religions.

Q.—Should you say that there is an unsocial principle in our Western people, which makes us so pluralistic, and that Eastern people are more sympathetic than we are?

A.—I think the Western people are more cruel, and the Eastern people have more mercy towards all beings. But that is simply because your civilisation is very much more recent. It takes time to make a thing come under the influence of mercy. You have a great deal of power, and the power of control of the mind has especially been very little practised. It will take time to make you gentle and good. This feeling tingles in every drop of blood in India. If I go to the villages to teach the people politics, they will not understand; but if I go to teach them Vedānta, they will say, "Now, Swami, you are all right". That Vairāgya, non-attachment, is everywhere in India, even today. We are very much degenerated now; but kings will give up their thrones and go about the country without anything.

In some places the common village-girl with her spinning-wheel says, "Do not talk to me of dualism; my spinning-wheel says 'Soham, Soham'—'I am He, I am He.'" Go and talk to these people, and ask them why it is that they speak so and yet kneel before that stone. They will say that with you religion means dogma, but with them realisation. "I will be a Vedantist", one of them will say, "only when all this has vanished, and I have seen the reality. Until then there is no difference between me and the ignorant. So I am using these stones and am going to temples, and so on, to come to realisation. I have heard, but I want to see and realise." "Different methods of speech, different manners of explaining the meaning of the scriptures—

these are only for the enjoyment of the learned, not for freedom" (Shankara). It is realisation which leads us to that freedom.

Q.—Is this spiritual freedom among the people consistent with attention to caste?

A.—Certainly not. They say there should be no caste. Even those who are in caste say it is not a very perfect institution. But they say, when you find us another and a better one, we will give it up. They say, what will you give us instead? Where is there no caste? In your nation you are struggling all the time to make a caste. As soon as a man gets a bag of dollars, he says, "I am one of the Four Hundred." We alone have succeeded in making a permanent caste. Other nations are struggling and do not succeed. We have superstitions and evils enough. Would taking the superstitions and evils from your country mend matters? It is owing to caste that three hundred millions of people can find a piece of bread to eat yet. It is an imperfect institution, no doubt. But if it had not been for caste, you would have had no Sanskrit books to study. This caste made walls, around which all sorts of invasions rolled and surged, but found it impossible to break through. That necessity has not gone yet; so caste remains. The caste we have now is not that of seven hundred years ago. Every blow has riveted it. Do you realise that India is the only country that never went outside of itself to conquer? The great emperor Ashoka insisted that none of his descendants should go to conquer. If people want to send us teachers, let them help, but not injure. Why should all these people come to conquer the Hindus? Did they do any injury to any nation? What little good they could do, they did for the world. They taught it science, philosophy, religion, and civilised the savage hordes of the earth. And this is the return—only murder and tyranny, and calling them heathen rascals. Look at the books written on India by Western people and at the stories of many travellers who go there; in retaliation for what injuries are these hurled at them?

Q.—What is the Vedantic idea of civilisation?

A.—You are philosophers, and you do not think that a bag of gold makes the difference between man and man. What is the value of all these machines and sciences? They have only one result: they spread knowledge. You have not solved the problem of want, but only made it keener. Machines do not solve the poverty question; they simply make men struggle the more. Competition gets keener. What value has nature in itself? Why do you go and build a monument to a man who sends electricity through a wire? Does not nature do that millions of times over? Is not everything already existing in nature? What is the value of your getting it? It is already there. The only value is that it makes this development. This universe is simply a gymnasium in which the soul is taking exercise; and after these exercises we become gods. So the value of everything is to be decided by how far it is a manifestation of God. Civilisation is the manifestation of that divinity in man.

Q.—Have the Buddhists any caste laws?

A.—The Buddhists never had much caste, and there are very few Buddhists in India. Buddha was a social reformer. Yet in Buddhistic countries I find that there have been strong attempts to manufacture caste, only they have failed. The Buddhists' caste is practically nothing, but they take pride in it in their own minds.

Buddha was one of the Sannyāsins of the Vedānta. He started a new sect, just as others are started even today. The ideas which now are called Buddhism were not his. They were much more ancient. He was a great man who gave the ideas power. The unique element in Buddhism was its social element. Brahmins and Kshatriyas have always been our teachers, and most of the Upanishads were written by Kshatriyas, while the ritualistic portions of the Vedas came from the Brahmins. Most of our great teachers throughout India have been Kshatriyas, and were always universal in their teachings; whilst the Brāhmana prophets with two exceptions were very exclusive. Rāma, Krishna, and Buddha—worshipped as Incarnations of God—were Kshatriyas.

Q.—Are sects, ceremonies, and scriptures helps to realisation?

A.—When a man realises, he gives up everything. The various sects and ceremonies and books, so far as they are the means of arriving at that point, are all right. But when they fail in that, we must change them. "The knowing one must not despise the condition of those who are ignorant, nor should the knowing one destroy the faith of the ignorant in their own particular method, but by proper action lead them and show them the path to come to where he stands." (Gitā, III. 26).

Q.—How does the Vedānta explain individuality and ethics?

A.—The real individual is the Absolute; this personalisation is through Māyā. It is only apparent; in reality it is always the Absolute. In reality there is one, but in Māyā it is appearing as many. In Māyā there is this variation. Yet even in this Māyā there is always the tendency to get back to the One, as expressed in all ethics and all morality of every nation, because it is the constitutional necessity of the soul. It is finding its oneness; and this struggle to find this oneness is what we call ethics and morality. Therefore we must always practise them.

Q.—Is not the greater part of ethics taken up with the relation between individuals?

A.—That is all it is. The Absolute does not come within Māyā.

Q.—You say the individual is the Absolute, and I was going to ask you whether the individual has knowledge.

A.—The state of manifestation is individuality, and the light in that state is what we call knowledge. To use, therefore, this term *knowledge* for the light of the Absolute is not precise, as the absolute state transcends relative knowledge.

Q.—Does it include it?

A.—Yes, in this sense. Just as a piece of gold can be changed into all sorts of coins, so with this. The state can be broken up into all sorts of knowledge. It is the state of superconsciousness, and includes both consciousness and unconsciousness. The man who attains that state has all that we call knowledge. When he wants to realise that consciousness of knowledge, he has to go a step lower. Knowledge is a lower state; it is only in Māyā that we can have knowledge.

Answers and Selections.

1. PERSONALLY I take as much of the Vedas as agrees with reason. Parts of the Vedas are apparently contradictory. They are not considered as inspired in the Western sense of the word, but as the sum total of the knowledge of God, omniscience. This knowledge comes out at the beginning of a cycle and manifests itself; and when the cycle ends, it goes down into minute form. When the cycle is projected again, that knowledge is projected again with it. So far the theory is all right. But that only these books which are called the Vedas are His knowledge is mere sophistry. Manu says in one place that that part of the Vedas which agrees with reason is the Vedas, and nothing else. Many of our philosophers have taken this view.

2. All the criticism against the Advaita philosophy can be summed up in this, that it does not conduce to sense-enjoyments; and we are glad to admit that.

3. The Vedānta system begins with tremendous pessimism, and ends with real optimism. We deny the sense-optimism but assert the real optimism of the Supersensuous. That real happiness is not in the senses but above the senses; and it is in every man. The sort of optimism which we see in the world is what will lead to ruin through the senses.

4. Abnegation has the greatest importance in our philosophy. Negation implies affirmation of the Real Self. The Vedānta is pessimistic so far as it negatives the world of the senses, but it is optimistic in its assertion of the real world.

5. Of all the scriptures of the world it is the Vedas alone that declare that even the study of the Vedas is secondary. The real study is "that by which we *realise* the Unchangeable". And that is neither reading, nor believing, nor reasoning, but superconscious perception, or Samādhi.

6. What is the cause of Māyā (illusion)? The question has been asked for the last three thousand years; and the only answer is: when the world is able to formulate a logical question, we shall answer it. The question is contradictory. Our position is that the Absolute has become this relative only apparently, that the Unconditioned has become the conditioned only in Māyā. By the very admission of the Unconditioned, we admit that the Absolute cannot be acted upon by anything else. It is uncaused, which means that nothing outside Itself can act upon It. First of all, if It is unconditioned, It cannot have been acted upon by anything else. In the Unconditioned there cannot be time, space, or causation. That granted your question will be: "What caused that which cannot be caused by anything to be changed into this?" Your question is only possible in the conditioned. But you take it out of the conditioned, and want to ask it in the Unconditioned. Only when the Unconditioned becomes conditioned, and space, time, and causation come in, can the question be asked. We can only say ignorance makes the illusion. The question is impossible. Nothing can have worked on the Absolute. There was no cause. Not that we do not know, or that we are ignorant; but It is above knowledge, and cannot be brought down to the plane of knowledge. We can use the words, "I do not know" in two senses. In one way, they mean that we are lower than knowledge, and in the other way, that the thing is above knowledge. The X-rays have become known now. The very causes of these are disputed, but we are sure that we shall know them. Here we can say we do not know about the X-rays.

But about the Absolute we cannot know. In the case of the X-rays we do not know, although they are within the range of knowledge; only we do not know them yet. But, in the other case, It is so much beyond knowledge that It ceases to be a matter of knowing. "By what means can the Knower be known?" You are always yourself and cannot objectify yourself. This was one of the arguments used by our philosophers to prove immortality. If I try to think I am lying dead, what have I to imagine? That I am standing and looking down at myself, at some dead body. So that I cannot objectify myself.

7. Evolution. In the matter of the projection of Ākāsha and Prāna into manifested form and the return to fine state, there is a good deal of similarity between Indian thought and modern science. The moderns have their evolution, and so have the Yogis. But I think that the Yogis' explanation of evolution is the better one. "The change of one species into another is attained by the infilling of nature." The basic idea is that we are changing from one species to another, and that man is the highest species. Patanjali explains this "infilling of nature" by the simile of peasants irrigating fields. Our education and progression simply mean taking away the obstacles, and by its own nature the divinity will manifest itself. This does away with all the struggle for existence. The miserable experiences of life are simply in the way, and can be eliminated entirely. They are not necessary for evolution. Even if they did not exist, we should progress. It is in the very nature of things to manifest themselves. The momentum is not from outside, but comes from inside. Each soul is the sum total of the universal experiences already coiled up there; and of all these experiences, only those will come out which find suitable circumstances. So the external things can only give us the environments. These competitions and struggles and evils that we see are not the effect of the involution or the cause, but they are in the way. If they did not exist, still man would go on and evolve as God, because it is the very nature of that God to come out and manifest Himself. To my mind this seems very hopeful, instead of that horrible idea of competition. The more I study history, the more I find that idea to be wrong. Some say that if man did not fight with man, he would not progress. I also used to think so; but I find now

that every war has thrown back human progress by fifty years instead of hurrying it forwards. The day will come when men will study history from a different light and find that competition is neither the cause nor the effect, simply a thing on the way, not necessary to evolution at all. The theory of Patanjali is the only theory I think a rational man can accept. How much evil the modern system causes! Every wicked man has a license to be wicked under it. I have seen in this country (America) physicists who say that all criminals ought to be exterminated and that that is the only way in which criminality can be eliminated from society. These environments can hinder, but they are not necessary to progress. The most horrible thing about competition is that one may conquer the environments, but that where one may conquer, thousands are crowded out. So it is evil at best. That cannot be good which helps only one and hinders the majority. Patanjali says that these struggles remain only through our ignorance, and are not necessary, and are not part of the evolution of man. It is just our impatience which creates them. We have not the patience to go and work our way out. For instance, there is a fire in a theatre, and only a few escape. The rest in trying to rush out crush one another down. That crush was not necessary for the salvation of the building nor of the two or three who escaped. If all had gone out slowly, not one would have been hurt. That is the case in life. The doors are open for us, and we can all get out without the competition and struggle; and yet we struggle. The struggle we create through our own ignorance, through impatience; we are in too great a hurry. The highest manifestation of strength is to keep ourselves calm and on our own feet.

8. Each soul is a circle. The centre is where the body is, and the activity is manifested there. You are omnipresent, though you have the consciousness of being concentrated in only one point. That point has taken up particles of matter and formed them into a machine to express itself. That through which it expresses itself is called the body. You are everywhere. When one body or machine fails you, the centre moves on and takes up other particles of matter, finer or grosser, and works through them. Here is man. And what is God? God is a circle with circumference nowhere and centre everywhere.

Every point in that circle is living, conscious, active, and equally working. With our limited souls only one point is conscious, and that point moves forward and backward.

9. The soul is a circle whose circumference is nowhere (limitless), but whose centre is in some body. Death is but a change of centre. God is a circle whose circumference is nowhere, and whose centre is everywhere. When we can get out of the limited centre of body, we shall realise God, our true Self.

10. Each soul is potentially divine. The goal is to manifest this Divinity within by controlling nature, external and internal. Do this either by work, or worship, or psychic control, or philosophy—by one, or more, or all of these—and be free. This is the whole of religion. Doctrines, or dogmas, or rituals, or books, or temples, or forms, are but secondary details.

11. Jnāna (knowledge) is "creedlessness"; but that does not mean that it despises creeds. It only means that a stage above and beyond creeds has been gained. The Jnāni (true philosopher) strives to destroy nothing but to help all. All rivers roll their waters into the sea and become one. So all creeds should lead to Jnāna and become one.

Jnāna teaches that the world should be renounced but not on that account abandoned. To live in the world and not to be of it is the true test of renunciation.

12. The Vedantist says that a man is neither born nor dies nor goes to heaven, and that reincarnation is really a myth with regard to the soul. The example is given of a book being turned over. It is the book that evolves, not the man. Every soul is omnipresent, so where can it come or go? These births and deaths are changes in nature which we are mistaking for changes in us.

13. Reincarnation is the evolution of nature and the manifestation of the God within.

14. The Vedānta says that each life is built upon the past, and that when we can look back over the whole past we are free. The desire to be free will take the form of a religious disposition from childhood. A few years will, as it were, make all truth clear to one. After leaving this life, and while waiting for the next, a man is still in the phenomenal.

15. The struggle never had meaning for the man who is free. But for us it has a meaning, because it is name-and-form that creates the world.

16. I cannot see how it can be otherwise than that all knowledge is stored up in us from the beginning. If you and I are little waves in the ocean, then that ocean is the background.

17. We would describe the soul in these words: "This soul the sword cannot cut, nor the spear pierce; the fire cannot burn nor water melt it; indestructible, omnipresent is this soul. Therefore weep not for it."

If it has been very bad, we believe that it will become good in the time to come. The fundamental principle is that there is eternal freedom for every one. Every one must come to it. We have to struggle, impelled by our desire to be free. Every other desire but that to be free is illusive. Every good action, the Vedantist says, is a manifestation of that freedom.

I do not believe that there will come a time when all the evil in the world will vanish. How could that be? This stream goes on. Masses of water go out at one end, but masses are coming in at the other end.

The Vedānta says that you are pure and perfect, and that there is a state beyond good and evil, and that is your own nature. It is higher even than good. Good is only a lesser differentiation than evil.

18. We have no theory of evil. We call it ignorance.

19. So far as it goes, all dealing with other people, all ethics, is in the phenomenal world. As a most complete statement of truth, we would not think of applying such things as ignorance to God. Of Him we say that He is Existence, Knowledge, and Bliss Absolute. Every effort of thought and speech will make the Absolute phenomenal and break Its character.

20. There is one thing to be remembered: that the assertion—I am God—cannot be made with regard to the sense-world. If you say in the sense-world that you are God, what is to prevent your doing wrong? So the affirmation of your divinity applies only to the noumenal. If I am God, I am beyond the tendencies of the senses and will not do evil. Morality of course is not the goal of man, but the means through which this freedom is attained. The Vedānta says that Yoga is one way that makes men realise this divinity. The Vedānta says this is done by the realisation of the freedom within and that everything will give way to that. Morality and ethics will all range themselves in their proper places.

21. We have a place for struggle in the Vedānta, but not for fear. All fears will vanish when you begin to assert your own nature. If you think that you are bound, bound you will remain. If you think you are free, free you will be.

22. That sort of freedom which we can feel when we are yet in the phenomenal is a glimpse of the real but not yet the real.

23. There is really no difference between matter, mind, and Spirit. They are only different phases of experiencing the One. This very world is seen by the five senses as matter, by the very wicked as hell, by the good as heaven, and by the perfect as God.

24. The Vedānta recognises the reasoning power of man a good deal, although it says there is something higher than intellect; but the road lies through intellect.

25. If we can stop all thought, then we know that we are beyond thought. We come to this by negation. When every phenomenon has been negatived, whatever remains, that is It. That cannot be expressed, cannot be manifested, because the manifestation will be, again, will.

26. It is true that we create a system, but we have to admit that it is not perfect, because the reality must be beyond all systems. We are ready to compare it with other systems and are ready to show that this is the only rational system that can be; but it is not perfect, because reason is not perfect. It is, however, the only possible rational system that the human mind can conceive.

It is true to a certain extent that a system must disseminate itself to be strong. No system has disseminated itself so much as the Vedānta. It is the personal contact that teaches even now. A mass of reading does not make men; those who were real men were made so by personal contact. It is true that there are very few of these real men, but they will increase. Yet you cannot believe that there will come a day when we shall all be philosophers. We do not believe that there will come a time when there will be all happiness and no unhappiness.

27. The Vedānta philosophy is the foundation of Buddhism and everything else in India; but what we call the Advaita philosophy of

the modern school has a great many conclusions of the Buddhists. Of course, the Hindus will not admit that—that is the orthodox Hindus, because to them the Buddhists are heretics. But there is a conscious attempt to stretch out the whole doctrine to include the heretics also.

28. The Vedānta has no quarrel with Buddhism. The idea of the Vedānta is to harmonise all. With the Northern Buddhists we have no quarrel at all. But the Burmese and Siamese and all the Southern Buddhists say that there is a phenomenal world, and ask what right we have to create a noumenal world behind this. The answer of the Vedānta is that this is a false statement. The Vedānta never contended that there was a noumenal and a phenomenal world. There is one. Seen through the senses it is phenomenal, but it is really the noumenal all the time. The man who sees the rope does not see the snake. It is either the rope or the snake, but never the two. So the Buddhistic statement of our position, that we believe there are two worlds, is entirely false. They have the right to say it is the phenomenal if they like, but no right to contend that other men have not the right to say it is the noumenal.

29. Will. Buddhism does not want to have anything except phenomena. In phenomena alone is desire. It is desire that is creating all this. Modern Vedantists do not hold this at all. We say there is something which has become the will. Will is a manufactured something, a compound, not a "simple". There cannot be any will without an external object. We see that the very position that will created this universe is impossible. How could it? Have you ever known will without external stimulus? Desire cannot arise without stimulus, or in modern philosophic language, of nerve stimulus. Will is a sort of reaction of the brain, what the Sânkhya philosophers call Buddhi. This reaction must be preceded by action, and action presupposes an external universe. When there is no external universe, naturally there will be no will; and yet, according to your theory, it is will that created the universe. Who creates the will? Will is coexistent with the universe. Will is one phenomenon caused by the same impulse which created the universe. But philosophy must

not stop there. Will is entirely personal; therefore we cannot go with Schopenhauer at all. Will is a compound—a mixture of the internal and the external. Suppose a man were born without any senses, he would have no will at all. Will requires something from outside, and the brain will get some energy from inside; therefore will is a compound, as much a compound as the wall or anything else. We do not agree with the will-theory of these German philosophers at all. Will itself is phenomenal and cannot be the Absolute. It is one of the many projections. There is something which is not will, but is manifesting itself as will. That I can understand. But that will is manifesting itself as everything else, I do not understand, seeing that we cannot have any conception of will, as separate from the universe. When that something which is freedom becomes will, it is caused by time, space, and causation. Take Kant's analysis. Will is within time, space, and causation. Then how can it be the Absolute? One cannot will without willing in time.

30. We cannot bring it to sense demonstration that Brahman is the only real thing; but we can point out that this is the only conclusion that one can come to. For instance, there must be this oneness in everything, even in common things. There is the human generalisation, for example. We say that all the variety is created by name and form; yet when we want to grasp and separate it, it is nowhere. We can never see name or form or causes standing by themselves. So this phenomenon is Māyā—something which depends on the noumenon and apart from it has no existence. Take a wave in the ocean. That wave exists so long as that quantity of water remains in a wave form; but as soon as it goes down and becomes the ocean, the wave ceases to exist. But the whole mass of water does not depend so much on its form. The ocean remains, while the wave form becomes absolute zero.

31. The real is one. It is the mind which makes it appear as many. When we perceive the diversity, the unity has gone; and as soon as we perceive the unity, the diversity has vanished. Just as in everyday life, when you perceive the unity, you do not perceive the

diversity. At the beginning you start with unity. It is a curious fact that a Chinaman will not know the difference in appearance between one American and another; and you will not know the difference between different Chinamen.

32. It can be shown that it is the mind which makes things knowable. It is only things which have certain peculiarities that bring themselves within the range of the known and knowable. That which has no qualities is unknowable. For instance, there is some external world, X, unknown and unknowable. When I look at it, it is X plus mind. When I want to know the world, my mind contributes three quarters of it. The internal world is Y plus mind, and the external world X plus mind. All differentiation in either the external or internal world is created by the mind, and that which exists is unknown and unknowable. It is beyond the range of knowledge, and that which is beyond the range of knowledge can have no differentiation. Therefore this X outside is the same as the Y inside, and therefore the real is one.

33. The Personal God is the same Absolute looked at through the haze of Māyā. When we approach Him with the five senses, we can see Him only as the Personal God. The idea is that the Self cannot be objectified. How can the Knower know Itself? But It can cast a shadow, as it were, if that can be called objectification. So the highest form of that shadow, that attempt at objectifying Itself, is the Personal God. The Self is the eternal subject, and we are struggling all the time to objectify that Self. And out of that struggle has come this phenomenal universe and what we call matter, and so on. But these are very weak attempts, and the highest objectification of the Self possible to us is the Personal God. This objectification is an attempt to reveal our own nature. According to the Sānkhya, nature is showing all these experiences to the soul, and when it has got real experience it will know its own nature. According to the Advaita Vedantist, the soul is struggling to reveal itself. After long struggle, it finds that the subject must always remain the subject; and then begins non-attachment, and it becomes free.

When a man has reached that perfect state, he is of the same nature as the Personal God. "I and my Father are one." He knows that he is one with Brahman, the Absolute, and projects himself as the Personal God does. He plays—as even the mightiest of kings may sometimes play with dolls.

34. Some imaginations help to break the bondage of the rest. The whole universe is imagination, but one set of imaginations will cure another set. Those that tell us that there is sin and sorrow and death in the world are terrible. But the other set—thou art holy, there is God, there is no pain—these are good, and help to break the bondage of the others. The highest imagination that can break all the links of the chain is that of the Personal God.

35. Now and then we know a moment of supreme bliss, when we ask nothing, give nothing, know nothing but bliss. Then it passes, and we again see the panorama of the universe moving before us; and we know that it is but a mosaic work set upon God, who is the background of all things.

The Vedānta teaches that Nirvāna can be attained here and now, that we do not have to wait for death to reach it. Nirvāna is the realisation of the Self; and after having once known that, if only for an instant, never again can one be deluded by the mirage of personality. Having eyes, we must see the apparent, but all the time we know what it is; we have found out its true nature. It is the screen that hides the Self, which is unchanging. The screen opens, and we find the Self behind it. All change is in the screen. In the saint the screen is thin, and the reality can almost shine through. In the sinner the screen is thick, and we are liable to lose sight of the truth that the Ātman is there, as well as behind the saint's screen. When the screen is wholly removed, we find it really never existed—that we were the Ātman and nothing else, even the screen is forgotten.

36. The two phases of this distinction in life are—first, that the man who knows the real Self, will not be affected by anything; secondly, that that man alone can do good to the world. That man alone will have seen the real motive of doing good to others, because there is only one, it cannot be called egoistic, because that would be differentiation. It is the only selflessness. It is the perception of the universal, not of the individual. Every case of love and sympathy is an assertion of this universal. "Not I, but thou." Help another because you are in him and he is in you, is the philosophical way of putting it. The real Vedantist alone will give up his life for a fellow-man without any compunction, because he knows he will not die. As long as there is one insect left in the world, he is living; as long as one mouth eats, he eats. So he goes on doing good to others; and is never hindered by the modern ideas of caring for the body. When a man reaches this point of abnegation, he goes beyond the moral struggle, beyond everything. He sees in the most learned priest, in the cow, in the dog, in the most miserable places, neither the learned man, nor the cow, nor the dog, nor the miserable place, but the same divinity manifesting itself in them all. He alone is the happy man; and the man who has acquired that sameness has, even in this life, conquered all existence. God is pure; therefore such a man is said to be living in God. Jesus says, "Before Abraham was, I am." That means that Jesus and others like him are free spirits; and Jesus of Nazareth took human form, not by the compulsion of his past actions, but just to do good to mankind. It is not that when a man becomes free, he will stop and become a dead lump; but he will be more active than any other being, because every other being acts only under compulsion, he alone through freedom.

37. Individuality. If we are inseparable from God, have we no individuality? Oh, yes: that is God. Our individuality is God. This is not the individuality you have now; you are coming towards that. Individuality means what cannot be divided. How can you call this individuality? One hour you are thinking one way, and the next hour another way, and two hours after, another way. Individuality is that which changes not—is beyond all things, changeless. It would be tremendously dangerous for this state to remain in eternity, because

then the thief would always remain a thief and the blackguard a blackguard. If a baby died, he would have to remain a baby. The real individuality is that which never changes and will never change; and that is the God within us.

38. God does not reason. Why should you reason if you know? It is a sign of weakness that we have to go on crawling like worms to get a few facts, and then the whole thing tumbles down again. The Spirit is reflected in mind and in everything. It is the light of the Spirit that makes the mind sentient. Everything is an expression of the Spirit; the minds are so many mirrors. What you call love, fear, hatred, virtue, and vice are all reflections of the Spirit. When the reflector is base, the reflection is bad.

39. We have been low animals once. We think they are something different from us. I hear, Western people say, "The world was created for us." If tigers could write books, they would say, man was created for them and that man is a most sinful animal, because he does not allow him (the tiger) to catch him easily. The worm that crawls under your feet today is a God to be.

40. I disagree with the idea that freedom is obedience to the laws of nature. I do not understand what it means. According to the history of human progress, it is disobedience to nature that has constituted that progress. It may be said that the conquest of lower laws was through the higher. But even there, the conquering mind was only trying to be free; and as soon as it found that the struggle was also through law, it wanted to conquer that also. So the ideal was freedom in every case. The trees never disobey law. I never saw a cow steal. An oyster never told a lie. Yet they are not greater than man. This life is a tremendous assertion of freedom; and this obedience to law, carried far enough, would make us simply matter—either in society, or in politics, or in religion. Too many laws are a sure sign of death. Wherever in any society there are too many laws, it is a sure sign that that society will soon die. If you study the characteristics of India,

you will find that no nation possesses so many laws as the Hindus, and national death is the result. But the Hindus had one peculiar idea—they never made any doctrines or dogmas in religion; and the latter has had the greatest growth. Eternal law cannot be freedom, because to say that the eternal is inside law is to limit it.

41. There is no purpose in view with God, because if there were some purpose, He would be nothing better than a man. Why should He need any purpose? If He had any, He would be bound by it. There would be something besides Him which was greater. For instance, the carpet-weaver makes a piece of carpet. The idea was outside of him, something greater. Now where is the idea to which God would adjust Himself? Just as the greatest emperors sometimes play with dolls, so He is playing with this nature; and what we call law is this. We call it law, because we can see only little bits which run smoothly. All our ideas of law are within the little bit. It is nonsense to say that law is infinite, that throughout all time stones will fall. If all reason be based upon experience, who was there to see if stones fell five millions of years ago? So law is not constitutional in man. It is a scientific assertion as to man that where we begin, there we end. As a matter of fact, we get gradually outside of law, until we get out altogether, but with the added experience of a whole life. In God and freedom we began, and freedom and God will be the end. These laws are in the middle state through which we have to pass. Our Vedānta is the assertion of freedom always. The very idea of law will frighten the Vedantist; and eternal law is a very dreadful thing for him, because there would be no escape. If there is to be an eternal law binding him all the time, where is the difference between him and a blade of grass? We do not believe in that abstract idea of law.

42. We say that it is freedom that we are to seek, and that that freedom is God. It is the same happiness as in everything else; but when man seeks it in something which is finite, he gets only a spark of it. The thief when he steals gets the same happiness as the man who finds it in God; but the thief gets only a little spark with a mass of misery. The real happiness is God. Love is God, freedom is God;

and everything that is bondage is not God.

43. The real Existence is without manifestation. We cannot conceive It, because we should have to conceive through the mind, which is itself a manifestation. Its glory is that It is inconceivable. We must remember that in life the lowest and highest vibrations of light we do not see, but they are the opposite poles of existence. There are certain things which we do not know now, but which we can know. It is due to our ignorance that we do not know them. There are certain things which we can never know, because they are much higher than the highest vibrations of knowledge. But we are the Eternal all the time, although we cannot know it. Knowledge will be impossible there. The very fact of the limitations of the conception is the basis for its existence. For instance, there is nothing so certain in me as my Self; and yet I can only conceive of it as a body and mind, as happy or unhappy, as a man or a woman. At the same time, I try to conceive of it as it really is and find that there is no other way of doing it but by dragging it down; yet I am sure of that reality. "No one, O beloved, loves the husband for the husband's sake, but because the Self is there. It is in and through the Self that she loves the husband. No one, O beloved, loves the wife for the wife's sake, but in and through the Self." And that Reality is the only thing we know, because in and through It we know everything else; and yet we cannot conceive of It. How can we know the knower? If we knew It, It would not be the knower, but the known; It would be objectified.

44. We need reason to drive out all the old superstitions; and what remains is Vedantism. There is a beautiful Sanskrit poem in which the sage says to himself: "Why weepest thou, my friend? There is no fear nor death for thee. Why weepest thou? There is no misery for thee, for thou art like the infinite blue sky, unchangeable in thy nature. Clouds of all colours come before it, play for a moment, and pass away; it is the same sky. Thou hast only to drive away the clouds." We have to open the gates and clear the way. The water will rush in and fill in by its own nature, because it is there already.

45. Man is a good deal conscious, partly unconscious, and there is a possibility of getting beyond consciousness. It is only when we become *men* that we can go beyond all reason. The words *higher* or *lower* can be used only in the phenomenal world. To say them of the noumenal world is simply contradictory, because there is no differentiation there. Man-manifestation is the highest in the phenomenal world. The Vedantist says he is higher than the Devas. The gods will all have to die and will become men again, and in the man-body alone they will become perfect.

46. Man has freedom already, but he will have to discover it. He has it, but every moment forgets it. That discovering, consciously or unconsciously, is the whole life of every one. But the difference between the sage and the ignorant man is that one does it consciously and the other unconsciously. Every one is struggling for freedom—from the atom to the star. The ignorant man is satisfied if he can get freedom within a certain limit—if he can get rid of the bondage of hunger or of being thirsty. But that sage feels that there is a stronger bondage which has to be thrown off. He would not consider the freedom of the Red Indian as freedom at all.

47. According to our philosophers, freedom is the goal. Knowledge cannot be the goal, because knowledge is a compound. It is a compound of power and freedom, and it is freedom alone that is desirable. That is what men struggle after. Simply the possession of power would not be knowledge. For instance, a scientist can send an electric shock to a distance of some miles; but nature can send it to an unlimited distance. Why do we not build statues to nature then? It is not law that we want but ability to break law. We want to be outlaws. If you are bound by laws, you will be a lump of clay. Whether you are beyond law or not is not the question; but the thought that we are beyond law—upon that is based the whole history of humanity. For instance, a man lives in a forest, and never has had any education or knowledge. He sees a stone falling down—a natural phenomenon happening—and he thinks it is freedom. He thinks it has a soul, and the central idea in that is freedom. But as soon as he knows that it

must fall, he calls it nature—dead, mechanical action. I may or may not go into the street. In that is my glory as a man. If I am sure that I must go there, I give myself up and become a machine. Nature with its infinite power is only a machine; freedom alone constitutes sentient life. The Vedānta says that the idea of the man in the forest is the right one; his glimpse is right, but the explanation is wrong. He holds to this nature as freedom and not as governed by law. Only after all this human experience we will come back to think the same, but in a more philosophical sense. For instance, I want to go out into the street. I get the impulse of my will, and then I stop; and in the time that intervenes between the will and going into the street, I am working uniformly. Uniformity of action is what we call law. This uniformity of my actions, I find, is broken into very short periods, and so I do not call my actions under law. I work through freedom. I walk for five minutes; but before those five minutes of walking, which are uniform, there was the action of the will, which gave the impulse to walk. Therefore man says he is free, because all his actions can be cut up into small periods; and although there is sameness in the small periods, beyond the period there is not the same sameness. In this perception of non-uniformity is the idea of freedom. In nature we see only very large periods of uniformity; but the beginning and end must be free impulses. The impulse of freedom was given just at the beginning, and that has rolled on; but this, compared with our periods, is much longer. We find by analysis on philosophic grounds that we are not free. But there will remain this factor, this consciousness that I am free. What we have to explain is, how that comes. We will find that we have these two impulsions in us. Our reason tells us that all our actions are caused, and at the same time, with every impulse we are asserting our freedom. The solution of the Vedānta is that there is freedom inside—that the soul is really free—but that that soul's actions are percolating through body and mind, which are not free.

48. As soon as we react, we become slaves. A man blames me, and I immediately react in the form of anger. A little vibration which he created made me a slave. So we have to demonstrate our freedom. They alone are the sages who see in the highest, most learned man, or

the lowest animal, or the worst and most wicked of mankind, neither a man nor a sage nor an animal, but the same God in all of them. Even in this life they have conquered relativity, and have taken a firm stand upon this equality. God is pure, the same to all. Therefore such a sage would be a living God. This is the goal towards which we are going; and every form of worship, every action of mankind, is a method of attaining to it. The man who wants money is striving for freedom—to get rid of the bondage of poverty. Every action of man is worship, because the idea is to attain to freedom, and all action, directly or indirectly, tends to that. Only, those actions that deter are to be avoided. The whole universe is worshipping, consciously or unconsciously; only it does not know that even while it is cursing, it is in another form worshipping the same God it is cursing, because those who are cursing are also struggling for freedom. They never think that in reacting from a thing they are making themselves slaves to it. It is hard to kick against the pricks.

49. If we could get rid of the belief in our limitations, it would be possible for us to do everything just now. It is only a question of time. If that is so, add power, and so diminish time. Remember the case of the professor who learnt the secret of the development of marble and who made marble in twelve years, while it took nature centuries.